fosebook: summer 20

*A collaborative project from the Flow
community of poets and art*

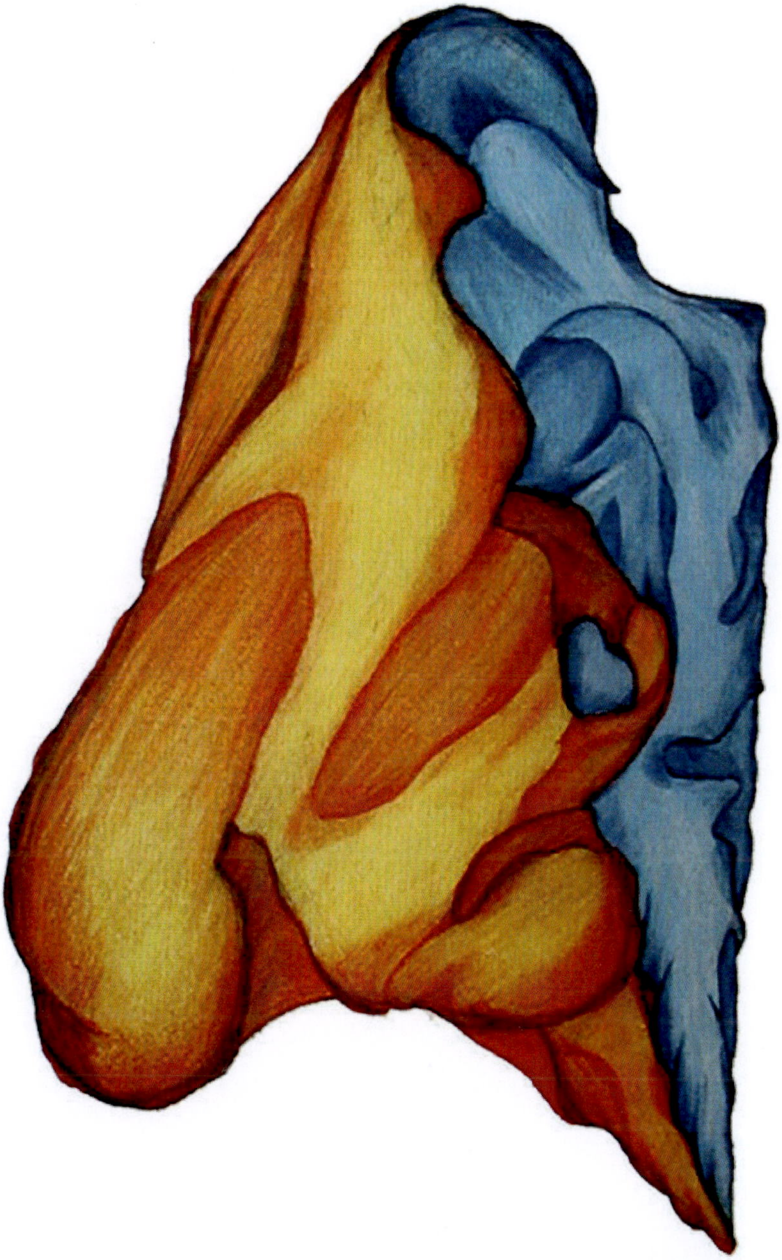

fosebook: summer 2010
was edited by Gerry Boyd, Megan Duffy, Anders Enochsson,
Jenny Enochsson and Francis Scudellari.

Individual pieces Copyright © 2010
by the respective creators

Design and Typesetting
Francis Scudellari

Front Cover Image:
Devi
Hand collage
by Charles Farrell

Title Page Image:
Fire and Ice
Color pencil on paper
by Francis Scudellari

Back Cover Image:
Expanse
Acrylic on canvas
by jb krost

ISBN: 978-0-557-50529-6

Printed in USA

Published June, 2010 by
fosebooks
http://flowersofsulfur.blogspot.com
email: fosebooks@gmail.com

Table of Contents

Words:

Images

Introduction

The collaborative blog *Flowers of Sulfur* is a breathing hole for unconventional, offbeat poetry and art. This publication contains pieces from poets and artists from all over the world who contribute and take part in this creative community.

Included in this edition of *fosebook* is work from nooshin azadi, Jeremy Blomberg, Gerry Boyd, Nikki Dahlke, Amanda Deo, Megan Duffy, Anders Enochsson, Jenny Enochsson, Charles Farrell, Neil Robert Graf, Christine Gram, John Grochalski, Harlequin, Pisces Iscariot, Per-Olav Johnson, timmy t jones, jb krost, Hannah Miet, rhoda penmarq, The Scrybe, Francis Scudellari, Thomas Sheridan and A'keith Walters.

Jenny Enochsson

refractor

a dapper man in retro redingote
throws a bratwurst boomerang
dented mirror and lead lumps
refraction of sunbeams
canal waves with grinded glass
a blue tit tries to drown sound
with his own cutting clinking

the wah-wah wood was shaved off
low-priced apartments were built
but the company did not bother about
laying even a lardy-dardy lawn
the recreation centre's frustrated fuzzbox
now fills the moats between the buildings
thunderbolts through nearby
dandelion leaves ahead of their time

coltsfoot sand water reservoir
a man on a bench reads a
second language book
a local semi-boozer also jazz flutist
in the spinous cells walks by
and says second-hand knowledge
you know my friend
ah abercrombie the other one smiles.

Endorphin Escalator

Cumulonimbus cloud champers
uncork: consumption crease
his soiled suit, nylon and spandex,
real polyurethane fiber frustration
with the foreman's pooch at his heels

Yes, the escalator, 2 meters per second
sagebrush filled handrails lag behind
alarmingly astigmatic shunting
thumping tambourine beaten steps

fosebook

Trainee thrall throws potash on
the already ultraviolet fire
radiative signage, infrared snow
neuron spiders thrive in the throng
always the same searchlight changes
cracking rope lights of white chocolate
spackling paste spreading like vitiligo

Santa is armed with Armagnac
he says kiss someone's feet under
supervision, silicon sinks in quick clay
it will pass, he hopes, soon
chromophobia, one single match left.

wishy-washy

city field hares starlings and borzoi fop
a saturated curaçao-blue sky with
heliotrope-green helium blimp
sponsored by company that holds
the record of reclaimed rulers

his terrier almost falls into the canal
cracking ice underbite but the animal
sinks his fangs into fake ermine fur
and shaggy calf belonging to a man who
is smoothing down his hair and insisting
on buying the pooch the master says
alright we are all sold sometimes
even when we say forget it

blinding black-body radiator fries
the yellow spot as if it was egg yolk
his cobalt gray often magnetic irises
he used to regard total opacity as
the ideal existence but now finds a
vitreous body's inside too wishy-washy
instead drawn to the husky light
of a geastrum rufescens.

Rutabaga Head
Color pencil on paper
by Francis Scudellari

bluing

white wine, eh, it is really yellowish-green
like liquidambar bloom bile or diacetyl
depending on the day delicious taste of
corrosively unripe banana stinging nettle
lemon marmalade butyl rubber roses
räkel's billiard ball of whining gristly
phlegm coughed up in his kitchen with
augustine a breeze below the window
the sun's shining corona on the walls
dissolving shellac on bare feet

the tap water calcareous starchy smoking
bluing spreading in oceans before coal rain
his pillow often smelled like soggy he-goat
he knew a woman who wanted new lungs
instead of a subsidized miniature oxygen bar
nearness to mine gave bone black saliva
this was not in the thirties the motion
is not linear it is helical.

feathers and jingling fringes

the tang-colored clouds seem like
marionettes dangling fleshy the sun like
a nude fruit rolled in tar and down
göran watches the street musicians
brass blow and dissonant dusty strings
dribbling gust streamer sound waves
a wood pigeon above a porous hill

llama in feathers and jingling fringes
teenage boy with eyes like green
swells of delighted spring dissolution
the boy walks like the lithe llama
jelly and slender muscles
terracotta sand and rubber gravel
a kid on a tight rope over the river
for the love of even-toed animals.

Neil Robert Graf

extinctionburst

what could they do what could they do. it wasn't like he was dead but he wasn't alive either what could they do. nothing would ever taste the same after that. we had all been wasted and bescrapped. some of us sat in metal chairs for long years. i spent the next stretch of time staining my skin and losing teeth one or two at a time to fists and amphetamines and blackness and bricks. with so much masonry one would think i would have built something. once i was aware of what it looked like to build. i left it behind. once the bright noises became quiet the wind carried away one grain of rock after another until silt was all i was. now and then there was sweetness. now and then. most of the taste was drying morningafter blood. most of it.

burn the works

yr foot whispered a smashed red aphid
dance / flirt / other noble occupations
accord with salty sardinians

a hundred thousand mile timebelt
resolved to attack synclines
it's no wonder

between recreational fireworks
& the real thing katyusha hellfire
it was still an eroded deposition.

recoilless

some tools cannot make me feel better now
leave the weapon unloaded stop driving

i think i need some more floor space; move the
bed i'm not really using it tonight

downtuned uptown negative compression
cropdusted yellow fingernail let ring

what's left to do but go for a hot flash
sugar rush did i say good night yeah blush.

epitaphii suspecta elogia

something about wednesday basement nights stirs
up a phlegmatic pneumonic darkness
sign in laundryworks says hey no dying
deter gent color in my mind and i
think about what it was like get it what

it was like exhaust
it was like hanging

light filtered in through the yellow slats and
frozen static splashed the sad pinpricked walls

awkward halfqueer lonely corner club
membership drive always
in full force psychic
influenza attacks fortnightly by

thriving in the trailers of the world like
mildew frosting a public shower wall

eleven thousand excuses to not
dream of irrelevant categories

can't this be made into something
that flashes hot on a flame and
goes down hot numb

listening to you roll your skyward eyes
is like stealing books
from a church my midsection stuck in the
broken and entered
door while i gather leatherbound copies
of the complete works
of charles dickens offcast to push off
an inland sandbar

running around with papers looking quite
important what could possibly go wrong
one hand on the grip with newly tightened
brakes the other palming burton's sourcebook
on christ allgoddamnedmighty am i a
nametagged boilerplated brother on a mission
or just another wired up
rodent wincing looking for a nudged bar.

Saturn Spring
Photograph
by Charles Farrell

spelt

words smell like breath
they launch off the deck
thrown by catapult
tongues burning blue fuels
after each thrust of
verb they are living
rockets striking ears

the words i write with
my hands are furrows
in black earth and
planted therein are
dicot leaves pushing
form from buried germs

the words that shake my
face are breaking fists
wet and sharp

the writing that cuts
is scorched plastic and
a belch of oilsmoke

and words cradle me
too old and tired
to run from my home.

Megan Duffy

Leadville Pantoum *—circa 1874*

little missy violet walks from the dance hall foyer
its hurdy gurdy sound detaches in tangents across the plain
Drone-strung, her torso waits for its player
A crib is a disheveled doldrum of human need

Its hurdy gurdy sound detaches in tangents across the plain
Somewhere beneath her breastbone a series of levers turn
A crib is a disheveled doldrum. Of human need:
the clanking-pocket gent, fierce gears in woolen trousers

Somewhere beneath her breastbone a series of levers turn
Beyond cracked walls, bursts of pewter snow
The clanking-pocket gent, fierce gears in woolen trousers—
after the dig, the sift, drip of the silvered tongue, there is this:

beyond the cracked walls, bursts of pewter snow
and her torso, a pliable instrument and white
After the dig, the sift, the drip of the silvered tongue, there is this:
a rosined heart pumps coniferous blood

and her torso, a pliable instrument and white
as powdered wind. Here within this branchless town
a rosined heart pumps coniferous blood—
Its hurdy gurdy sound detaches in tangents across the plain

Author's note: *Leadville, Colorado was the site of the 1874 American silver boom. As more and more fortune hunters descended on the area, the city of Leadville became known for its brothels and "Hurdy Gurdy Girls." A crib is 19th C. slang for a rented brothel room. Cribs were typically minuscule and windowless.*

The Honeymoon Tour

In Milan, the new bride
emerges from the hotel elevator
without her groom
(he waiting alone by the bar).
She turns her toes toward him,
heels clicking beneath her.

She is stopped by the hand of a man
Placed on the small of her back,
pulling her in to his roiling lips.
She cannot focus on the face at this
angle. He is one of the tour, she knows that.

You're beautiful, he steams
surprised by his own voice.
Her eyes find the floor as
a word surfaces in her mind.
The hand is removed.
He shifts away,
returns to his inebriated wife.

Outside, night.
North African prostitutes
haunt the frigid fields.
By morning,
only stiletto holes
filled with tongues of frost.

Bareness is the word.

      bareness.

Automatic Ballad for Jean Arp

Teller of found immensities:
abandoned bulb, abandoned bone
marble-lip, sound throat-less, free
great chunks of plastic: saxophone

Herder of cloudy Coquille thirst
or splintered wood, improbable blue
an accidental   automatic ego-quill
of unmeasured orange gutty stew

Star lust reeks in plastered blanc
unnoticed thumbtack   winking toad
crystal umbrage orbits thick
within otherwise worlds untold

Hard to get
Mixed media collage on canvas panel
by Nikki Dahlke

The Sunken Head Rears in Windows

a.
Once, in the apartment above Union Square, she threatened to push me out the window. She stood behind me, her arms locked around my shoulders like wet branches, like a lover but more so, closer, nearer. *You must move forward,* she said and used her mass to move me to the sill.
Because I knew her well, I slowly removed her arms and drew an alternative from her brain:
Let's make your poster of Sid Vicious into an oversized paper airplane. So we sent the dried-blood/black and white drone on a lazy spin over the Square, watching it briefly gain momentum as it sailed by the statue of Gandhi, grazing his baked-bean face, then landing in a crumple beneath a bench where city squirrels, ashen and overly-friendly, began to investigate the image of anarchy.

b.
We emerge from ourselves moment by moment.
Etching out our finer, crystalline shapes,
we release the vapors like shredded
skins of frost on double panes of glass.
It is happening always, as every moving
day of November is a little more December.

c.
Sucking on a Marlboro, up 5th Ave, every step I take I am farther from her: 17th, 18th, 19th, cross streets cross us here, there… she is behind me. My smoke sails backward into her eyes: *Reversals,* her reflection smoldering in storefronts. I reach the Flatiron where the center captures us in glass—we merge like binary stars, a bundle of smoke and past. When I skid around the corner of the ever-widening structure, she becomes lost, sunk in subway steam…

d.
Numbers are not to be trusted.
We become in letters, words, sentences
said, and broken, then said again, running on
and on and on the hour, by the hour, the seconds
are made of strung vowels, landmasses
of layered consonants. From these we form.
Numbers are not to be trusted:
they are voiceless.

e.
…but years and words later, I sit, facing a third-floor window. Below are tree tops— branches spread like neurons—ripped vein red. I see her behind me, my sunken-self, her smoked skin merging with the reflected blood of the maple. Closer, nearer.

f.
You must move forward,
we say.

A Proper Diagnosis
after Sarah Waters

1.

Then look again, my Dear Caroline.
The Little Stranger is outside the parlor,
clanging candlesticks against the balustrade.
She emerged in gusty soot the moment
you scolded the scullery maid
for leaving the boot-room strewn with straw.

Fire is not a trial worth tempting.
You have a weakness, Dear, like your
brother (now under the care of the Vicar of St. Albans).
The brandy is not this weakness; only
an amber mirror that shatters
down the throat.

2.

The Estate was broken shortly after the War, the second, the flamethrower, that
scorched the smutty skirts of London and menaced the greeny shires with invisible
smoke. There was no more room for such a pile in the Midlands where rural families
suddenly were in need of washrooms square gardens. And here it must be said that an
ancient home will become agitated when its foundation is threated. Pockets of air, filled
with things that have happened—like the dark space beneath the second floor landing
where a small boy once bounced a pig-skinned ball over and over and over as his
nursery-maid shouted for him from above—remain and beg attention in the silliest of
ways.

3.

Poor Roddy was never properly
held by his mother. That must account
for his abnormal admiration for the flame.
The touch of fire is like no other touch:
a blue kiss, a digging tongue
that rewrites the skin.
For the starved of love, a lick
of ember is the milky nipple
never pulled.
Poor boy. How he loved that
second floor landing, dark and
tight and warm like the red-lined
walls of flesh in which he began.

4.

A skull is really a mansion, isn't it? An estate with the most complex configuration of wings: branches and barnacles off-shooting in fissured currents from plate of bone to plate of bone. And all that meat in between where our full-length mirrors reflect every instance, every occurrence from pink unwinding to grey goodbye...

5.

...and the strangers that hide behind them,
and the strangers that move within them.

Handmaiden
Photograph
by Charles Farrell

timmy t jones

sis

sis was the town tramp
but she wasn't a bad kid
when the police brought her home in the morning
they always bought her an ice cream cone

the city was ringed with ice cream shops
and dairy whip stands too
in winter there was dunkin donuts
there was no escape

the red and blue lights of the police cars
blot out the milky way
you couldn't see the andromeda galaxy
even if the town had outskirts

officer stone was a jets fan
and wanted to move to oregon
officer mcgovern preferred the philadelphia eagles
and liked to take his three kids on picnics

they stood on the front porch
with the fog laughing silently behind them
and said, mr and mrs america
here is your wandering girl

at the beach

went to the beach
instead
of looking for a job

cold morning
no tourists
the waves are white

the foaming rocks
the hills
and the gray sky

clouds roll up
like limousines
waves crash and die

cold raindrops
riddle the sand
fur of a running cat

police car
stops for a hot dog
in the rain

running down the beach
the pit bull stops
shell of a manta ray

sky god - triumphant
sun god - devouring
sea goddess - forgotten

no more messages
but humans
still watch the waves

the hope of love dies hard
a sunset
infinitely prolonged

human hand
monster hand
above the waves

the great hand
of the sea and sky
no fingers

for thirty seconds
reality
called to me

reality is reality
and i'm
only myself

bulbous seaweed
ripped
from the ocean floor

i wanted to kill myself
i went and looked at the ocean
i felt better

waves
voices
waves

fine sand
across the muck
like frosting

green light/not really an american

she was one of those people you just like to be around.

she was one of the original five, or one of the original six. this fascinated me.

we were headed uptown to the airport. then she remembered frank or billy, he was like a
father or a brother to her. we went back downtown to look for him.

we split up to look for him. i was walking along a construction site and these punks
were laughing and coming toward me with plastic bags of blue paint. they were going to
paint me blue. somehow i got away.

we were going back uptown. she was driving. i thought, i'll never understand the traffic
in this town. the light was red. three guys came up behind us on the sidewalk, the two
on the outside holding up the one in the middle. he didn't look drunk, more like he was
spastic or had serious problems. they were laughing about something – "that sounds
like something you would hear at macdonalds". something about playing ball – i didn't

get it because i'm not a real american. the guy on the outside turned into a fish/basketball and floated on his back in the gutter.

the light turned green. i started to know it was a dream. i woke up. i never saw her again. i never knew who she was.

the wanderer

icy lights
behind black

glass. come on
buddy, you

have to go
someplace else

can i stay
until i

finish my
candy bar

let's go – now!
i went to
harvard, i'm
a teacher

at berkeley
the candy

bar's made of
coconut

it will freeze
and break my

teeth, all right
make it hard

on me, do
you really

want to make
me fill out

a report
and take you

downtown in
this weather?

then i won't
be your friend

any more
i went to

harvard. i'm
a science

professor
at berkeley

berkeley is
three thousand

miles away
i know, i.m

waiting for
the bus, but

i lost my
ticket, and
besides, you
are not a

real cop, just
a transit

cop, oh just
a transit

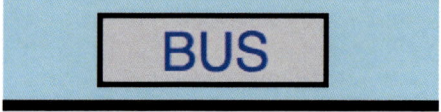

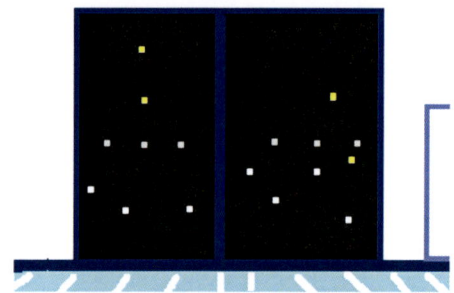

cop, and this
is what, your

private bed
room, icy

lights. sudden
blast of air

goodbye. lost
my ticket

raindrops

there is desperation
in the greenest trees
a secret conflagration
in the coolest breeze

the kitten at the window
the butterfly in the air
watch the raindrops follow
each other in despair

and when the leaves fall
yellow in the rain
the sidewalk hears them call
a whispered name

Gerry Boyd

to celebrate this time we've had together

i. resistance is futile in the face of crushing surf

when the timely spray leers a proper twelve o'clock
my etched face always bends towards the salty ocean
with the upright satisfaction of a quiet sandy satyr:

greens smashed by the green smashed in another giddy decade,
rise now smoothly as the sandy glass of tide-ripped bottles.

when the sun gives rise to the alto sand of sea-grass spring,
we can only sniff for the pounding waves that make us gyrate so.

eyes uncontrollably rivet the shine of a clinging maillot,
the pulsing jade of amulet that is our cherished sea-glass.

was it the teal that made it so?

ii. when you bought a black return, the station master giggled

the end of blank expression is pregnant with the eternal possibility
of small font timetables blurred in the black wash of anxious tears:

all aboard! all aboard! were we going somewhere? oh yes. we were.

then you bring in the comfy chair to stroke the sweet coffined coif-
salty hams on flocked upholstery only enhance the coughing fetish:

suppressing laughter is always laughing most dryly choked
when narrowing and distracted eyelids are least able to wetly thrill.

we wandered the twisty dead-end hallways
until the musty death of twisty wanderings,
announced the twisty death of musty wanderings:

our hotel proudly served the scarlet pepper goulash
in cobalt china bowls that skittered from the sideboard
like mutant mice desperately trying to please the dead.

this was before your lungs gasped the closing air

that was rancid in the claustrophobia of the alcove,
before we grasped the smoky closing of a velvet door:

I did not know the dead could have such hair.

iii. insipid murmurs about the cycle of life

each atom of the acidic raindrop that plagues you now
was a salty teardrop crusting on Cleopatra's cheek
when she stared into the desert and wondered why she cared,
when she stared into the swirling dust with bitter eyes of kohl
waiting for the brute that never comes:

so much for the stamped and signed postcards from the forum.

enjoy, if you can, a prophetic mixture of soot and salt,
arriving in your waiting box with so much postage due.

iv. after the storm we noticed broccoli treetops

pearls that hang from evergreens:

if only the afternoon would glimmer
like it did that day in shimmering August
when the rooftops angled against the sparrows
and the fear of flight became a silver possibility
that commoditized a pitiless sun
with terracotta arcs of blissful sienna
near a violet gate open and cascading
with a formal flood of planned wisteria.

yes, yes, you were there and jangled too.

v. in that day we welcomed boredom

a painted tunnel devoid of butterflies
can only give a sprayed and painful birth
to the luscious graffiti of orange and pearl:

come, she said, come play with me.

Angel Eyes
Photograph
by Charles Farrell

even enigmas deserve farewells

i. this was a journey I never intended

after the weeping bride was ushered from dust,
she came and returned,
through the bad hair infinities of catholic statues:

creepy, creepy, creepy.

and, then, she wrapped a lacquered box of ashen remains
into a lengthy scarf of lacy bone and fussy linen,

speaking that funny breath which only lives on widows—

I held my brotherly weep
through the ceremony of silly hats and silk,
through the chanting of a veil,
but released it gladly
for the scarlet processional
of black turned white:

but only
but only

because ten was ten on sale just now beneath keyser avenue
in an extraordinary discount on red hot sausages,

that barked surreal on that ordinary august day—

they were offered in scarlet hand on sidereal cardboard:

I could not suggest out loud while sweltering
through the summer sweat of tiny purple falcons
that esoteric naming was an unnatural act for me,
reserved so I thought, for that moment of grace,
when the pale monsignor and his swarthy minion

made the basilica of st. anne smoky fresh with myrrh.

having heard about this anne,
I decided to make a K-turn.

ii. every body comes from somewhere

fosebook

a grave observance of boneyard maintenance,
was softly trumped by blades sharpened but barely used
on the majestic green carpet so prophetically deaf
to a funereal gurgle that prospered on rhythmic hills:

she said lock, I said open—

this was the world before fire.

iii. the pressing reception of endless sorry

by you, I held a hand of scarlet,

rusty graves forming the flushed push of red parapets:

this is where our choices narrow into marshy deltas,

into the thin promise of a gaunt and yellowed family tree
and thirsty purple pistils with a perky greeting card font—

snookered by the scenic overlook that takes me hoom [sic].

this sweet low lumbering beneath a city of unexpected
charcoal cave-ins and the moaning black of carbondale.

the relish-drenched offering of discount dogs,

offered like anything else in life,
an end at the start and a start at the end.

I especially liked the corner cabinet of sacred oils
with its endless neon flashing:

save me is just so beatifying.

if we could only count the speckles

i. because there was no rain to soak us through

the timid beak of the bathing thrush
concentrically ripples the polished dapples.

the mirrored pool smirks beneath austere maples,
an intrusion of rust forcing the oxbow birth:

there is a current that knows its swirling mind
and will not bend to unbend the cowering mud.

six stark claws leave evidence of lather.

ii. each fluttering wing has a hidden story

one flashing swoop flips a visitation,
blackly tumbling a quilled re-division
for the fossilized flutter of a feathered bed.

latitudes where a fallen bud once made sense
seem to diminish in the gray uncertain moments
and the intoxicating orange of a crisply setting sun:

an idle counting of ones and twos and threes
reflects the breathy throbs of what might be:

an ironic ode to the ocher futilities of shale.

iii. into the quiet thrashing of languid dreams

each drooping laughing half-formed leaf
that spurts to flourish in early spring
becomes a sermon on the mount unheard.

each drip of sap a sticky tear
that runs through the maple eyes
of a world that will never bloom:

a cryptic euphoria that fails each breath
when the end of the clouds is grasped.

your mock apple pie is already being served.

Dream Door
Photograph
by Charles Farrell

dripping sweat into the crescent

i. bastet leered when you sanded the dog-star

the dynastic womb of your drooping limestone desire
had prickled the chipped tomb of my pharaonic intent
when the crescent dove flooded the canine drawl at dawn:

you can't be serious.

grrrr.

how many lascivious cones does it take to mold a croissant dominant,
patiently, into a steamy delta buttered by kohl black nightfall,
an empire once mummified in a chronic loss of apocryphal noses
hidden inside the starry rolls and ermine wraps of buttery resolution?

welcome, once again, to the boredom of eternity:

where the fuck is my cat?

ii. the secret ministry of frost is the first misdemeanor

you were caught by the generous green boughs of hemlock,
before the sacred teas had browned your crispy veins,
before you slept, awhile, in the scratchy embrace of velvet fingers-

misdemeanor the second:

before high-piled books, in charactery—

misdemeanor the third:

the lone and level sands stretch far away.

call me serial:
oops, I did it again,
but badly and out of time.

isn't it romantic?

iii. not a moment is ever wasted

always, but only in memory must we return

to the moments when the sleek quenching rain
abundantly splashed your freckled face and
unexpectedly gleamed the shimmery grain of alder beams
in that secret orange loft under the gauzy sun of winter
where bits of desiccated hay anointed drooping marigolds-

it was the day your eyes rolled, timelessly,
into the whiteness of tomorrow.

it was the day we died in parallel,
like all great lovers do:

what a pity to be born again.

It was along a river that I never heard

*"There are varied responses to the process of
socialization. Many acquiesce and replicate
with their children what their parents did to them.
Others do not. In clinical observation, we can oscillate
the difference."*
Thorsten Heisendykker, The Bland Mirror of the Medusa Ego

i. Once more, into that pesky garden

Prickly troubled being burst forth again
along the newly spaded furrow of jaded roses,
often bubbly wrapped as a hapless thorny stem
against the rubber boots of a tame green calf,
often pitched by the sleeping wight of life
or the soiling dreams of ever-blooming black:
yikes! the concrete square is so sweaty rich
with the capillary dew of bloody aspiration.

In the swampy mist a hunkered rail
quakes in mirth as the banshees wail:

a two-clawed braid of mossy twist
with elbows blue towards bluer sky
in a heathen dance of heathered mists.

And so it ends and so it begins.

ii. Climb every anthill until you reach

From the violet calm of my omega
I saw the alpha swirl of contenders
dissipate and cease to snarl at rivals.

I had a chartreuse tiffin with twin black straps
and a plastic zipper that never stuck
to carry fruits and nuts and yogurt:

persimmons and clementines mostly,
an occasional prickly pear—
blanched almonds and pistachios,
savory with the salt of the sea.

I watched your reflection
but the sun came out
and you went in
squeaking a hinge behind,

blankly.
I parked my aqua truck in a narrow space
and solved the white brick puzzle.

Cutting the deck with every breath,
was it brave, then, to draw another?

I spun with the cirrus in a fulcrum of air,
I spun with the mud that had clumped in your hair,
I spun and my eyes were white and nowhere.

And spun and spun, spun again.

Amanda Deo

Anna

She said *we're gonna sink or swim* and I was sittin' on the back porch watching the dog rich with the currency of squirrels. She was yelling at me from the kitchen window and I was gettin' pretty pissed off because driving a mail truck all day isn't all that glorious and neither is the castrato shriek from the window.

"What's your goddamn problem?" she said.

"Just let me stand next to your fire..." he sighed.

Get it Right

Watching *My Best Friend's Wedding* at
2am. Every time Julia opens her mouth I
know I've got to accept this, love.

Turning Twenty-Six

Turning twenty-six is boring. I've reached no milestones. I haven't influenced any one to do anything good. I'm a slave to the wage. I run around the office like I've got nothing better to do. I hate photocopiers and ink cartridges. I fake interest.

We fake love—

around midnight
when no one is
watching I coin
new phrases to
make myself
memorable and
click my fingers
snap them on
off beats to
Happy Birthday
to You.

Looking Through a Machine
Mixed media collage on canvas panel
by Nikki Dahlke

Hybrid

Je me souviens que né sous le lys, je croîs sous la rose.
(I remember that while I was born under the lily, I grew under the rose)

And that's just sort of how
it went for
years.

Champlain never saw
it coming.

First Trimester

She lost it. It
cried out of her.
Knocked off
its own perch.

Tumbled out. Legs like
tumbleweeds.

What have we lost here?

Too much.

Jeremy Blomberg

How We Understand Space

I slide between narrow rows of pines
crunching needles under soft feet
and note the paleness of the horizon
through green and tangled branches.

Christmas is all I smell:
eggnog, wrapping paper, chopped oak
burning a red flavor through the house.

I step past the framed columns of trees
and stand at the edge of a field;
the world looks broken from here,
caught under these dreary eyes,
frozen in shambles until the spring.

I wish I could speak of the sun—
registers shooting warm air into gloves,
the heat saving my hands for tomorrow.

Fingers now chilled numb by the wind
and pockets loaded with pine cones,
I call myself the walking tree
as I step through the empty field
pushing seeds into the snow and ice.

A quiet warmth sets through my veins
as the sap and dust sticks to my clothes
and nothing is left to do but wait;
out here, memories are never certain,
but maybe I will not die alone.

Stars are Stars
Acrylic on canvas
by Thomas Sheridan

It is Our Dreams that Scare Us

I fell asleep with something like love
sprinkled over my lips and throat
and watched as the sun slowly turned
into the soft glow of a second moon;
two nights now living above my head
I had no place to go for warmth, so I froze
and stared as the moons grew brighter
passing reflections back-and-forth
like two young flickering candles.

Faster and faster
the moons revolved around the earth
chasing one another as if they were old friends
reunited once again, yearning to be more than echoes
forgotten under my simple astonished gaze.
Faster and faster
the two began to gain speed, forming a new energy
that buckled my knees against its pressure,
and swallowed my ears under heavy dead tones.
Faster and faster
they continuously rotated around my being
consuming each one of my senses
until, finally, they disappeared,
stealing the light into a darkness where I did not exist,
seeking something I could not understand—
constellations were set free to scatter over my eyes,
and the sky was perfect for that moment.

Then, as if on cue,
I felt the earth tremble beneath my feet
as it opened a burning trench of mist,
spewing red-orange heat into the air;
afraid, I turned and ran
faster and faster
away from the blazing rays of light,
the crumbling pieces of dirt and rock.
The land quickly broke under my strides
and I fell through the world on my back,
flailing my useless arms
faster and faster
as if I still had a choice.

I awoke on a cold rock island
and asked the man standing before me,
"Could I have changed the sun?"

In the Evening

A thick honey stretches between parting lips,
and I have found time to live forever;
stuck to the final thoughts in a falling sun,
I strain young words for the rays to never fade—
never steal desires now baked too brittle
to whisper (as truths) over ears
hardened by sweet, aging lights.

Cold hands slide over cold hands:

      red smoke in our eyes,
      burnt tar in the air,
      a warm rain becomes mist.

The night will find us a constant winter
as we cannot change with the leaves,
left to simply soften and tear beneath the ice.
We will not gasp or breathe, but remember
warm shadows of a long burning sun.

Old Intentions Make Young Memories

We caught every glaring spark
chased from the embers
of our last campfire.
She, finely aged, burned
faster than I could taste
as we were both lit like two drinks
drenched in the flames of thought.
Closer than a friendly touch,
she wrapped her motherly arms
around the skinny in my shoulders
and whispered questions about what life meant
in the light of my blue eyes—
my eyes were so blue, her next baby
was going to have my eyes, because blue eyes
look beautiful on black babies. I agreed
all night to everything she said and touched:
the tips of my hair, edge of my ear, open spaces
between my chin and legs. I heard the word *love*
slide down the back of my head, dreaming
about her slightly wrinkled smile
the way blue jeans fit perfectly
around her waist, the loops around my fingers.
While I imagined this burning
translucent idea of us,
the fire fell into a pile of red

as the smoke twisted through her hair
blowing an airy future like ashes
into the squinting dawn.
Quickly fading,
she rose
and began a dance
between the fire and my eyes;
the sun
slowly rising behind the trees,
she danced
into the light, the blue, the smoke flavored taste
shifting side-to-side over my bare tongue.
Then, taking my hand
she placed it within soft, deep patterned palms,
and we walked into her house,
carefully stepping out of the night.

The Alchemist Outdoors

I bang my fists against an apple tree,
and pinecones crash down over my head
like the sporadic winds of consciousness
that I inhale to undo, understand and redo.

I hear a second voice slip through the branches
and watch as it changes leaves into words
hanging like fruit, hoping someone will taste.

I melt snow in my hands
        blow water into glass seeds
    then chew
the
    pieces
  into
        sand

but I cannot seem to make my space grow
or change—stubborn seasons revolve;
I want the sky to rain fire for months,
the lakes to boil before the ice,
and trees to burn leaves off their limbs.

I want to capture that second voice,
I want to destroy and recreate old times
that sound as if they just might understand
ideas on how to burn thoughts into gold.

Harlequin

Sequoia

Graceful visitors
hovering above ground, roots exposed
Unstable
in any language of certainty
(you) wouldn't stand a chance
singing solo
A cappella sighs
sustained in a generous space
choirs find connections
at the deep bedrock of longing
intertwining rides out the storms

Underground, overground
onslaughts
chime down
to murmuring dawn
landscapes awash
with tranquil brown puddles
deep enough for a dozen sparrows
their little brown bodies quickening
into spiky wetness
their waterplay a frolic of hops, chirps
and fluttering
unguarded vulnerability

Let's watch them for a few minutes, you say
and memory, being the carnal tether that it is,
calls me back to every shared heartbeat
Loving
how your strength resides in your unhurried watchfulness
a golden moment testimony
to the resilience of grass,
dandelions and groves
leaning into twilight
when everything has a chance to move

A Windswept House
Watercolour and ink on paper
by Thomas Sheridan

The Ravens of March
Watercolour & ink on paper ● *by Thomas Sheridan*

The Scrybe

Stasis

Rocking chair sway
Here I stand again
Glued to the highest point
Stuck once more at the zenith
Where lip presses firm against tile

Complicated elements
I have lost myself again
Silent at the pinnacle
Cool and snug at the summit
And I am unrecognisable and fractious and glib

Candelabra

Sugar topped sandcastle turret,
in a room where the evergreens grow
I'll take my seat by the window,
looking out at a blanket of snow

How inside of the glass is a shadow
full of mirrors, and portholes, and doors
Where the sunshine is crooked, and narrow
like the whispers she holds in her jaws

For in one of my earliest memories
beating down, with its tail on my lips
I was sat in the cove of a cup nest,
with a mouth full of feathers and fists

Girl to the North

Acrylic on canvas

by jb krost

A death of sorts
Two chipped fingernails
beneath the pillow
you gave me
last summer

You know the one,
duck down
And a picture of your
University
boat-race
across its bow

I'll make a believer of you yet
I'll leak and tear,
And cast it all out to sea

But by then
who knows?

Perhaps the realisation
that, like every good
garden,
this love needs
to be tended with care,

will have you swollen
and calling
my name.

Quarantine

To stand on the edge of a rock pool
and not actually jump in

To hold firm on the threshold
a voyeur refusing to enter

To eavesdrop on life itself
listening to all of its whispers
and unraveling all of its mysteries

But to never open up
and share the journey with others

M I double S

Lorelei,
I hear a whisper
on your breath

And the void
you left behind
is forever untying
all
my
ribbons

Down below
the confusion
is impossible to deny

But up here
reflection
is the only perspective

Dressing down,
a lesser sense of self
Faceless and hiding,
social constructs cast aside

Pressing the mortal mass together
Words uttered
from two lips twice denied

And
how can the sun dare to shine
when you are not here?

Christine Gram

senza ombrello

The headline read
Cold and a little humid... perfect for the super flu
Could have said,
The perfect weather to stay in bed
Or hide under your umbrella
Or the thoughts in your head
Whispers of snow
Breaths of ice
Wet the tracks, white the ties
Falling gently like rain, but lighter...
Lighter in layers
Of silk cotton and wool
Pulled from their beds
Spun woven and wrapped
Just to lift you up
When you find the weather
Senza ombrello

face of the earth

A left and a right and a left-hop-skip
I think I've gone and hopped right off it

I've let myself dive into the persistent cloud-cover,
feeling the gray and gloomy days.
While lush mountains with their woolly green coats
flock the sulking Shepard.
Who sits on her rock and consoles her heart
drawing rivers with a stick in the mud
You see, the earth and the rain are playing a game
coaxing this crab from her shell.
For sit long enough on the most comfortable rock
and your bony ass will get sore
And your numb bum and the soft filtered sun
will cause you to stretch and to eye (unawares)
Whereupon Mother Kesey and her gang of merry pranksters
Swiftly sneeze you into the sky.

Boundless • *Acrylic on canvas* • *by Thomas Sheridan*

dreams

I have dreams.
Dreams of scaling El Capitan
Clamped to the edge of the world,
Drifting at the edge of space.
Dreams of tall pines and sap on my fingers
The sting of scraped knees and my breath
Caught as we sway with the wind.
Or being old and weaving loose ends
The loose ends of a fortunate life.
Loose ends that slip into a comfortable knit
With an old friend with the right loose ends.
Dreams of being unknown
But knowing myself
Just driving off in a new direction
And being exactly what I feel like being.
Or spinning these things
Bits of death and love and reaching far places
With an unseen touch into the web.
Into the ebb, into the bed,
Into... and
Out of my head.
I will not live in dreams
But dreams are the thing.
The things that fill up the vast empty spaces
An oil that carries heat from the fire
To everything cold
To everything real.

sos

Stale peeps and Coco Wheats
Things that make my life complete
Shipped in a box across the blue
Can you wrap yourself up too?

twilight passages

the silence of the night lets my thoughts fall out before me
all that is rolled up safely on my back during the day
the music in "Dead Man's Chest" and Luca's lines recited for a play
He is a farmer in Happyland, full of happy animals.
Your voice, stronger now than the images that are there
I can hear my heart beating
and the sound of my smile when I hear you talking
the air rushing out when it hits me
I see all these things I'm supposed to do
all the elements of my life and dreams
as simple as the dotted pasture in Happyland
reduced to simple treasures in my pocket
collected on a barefoot walk through the fields
all the things that brightened my eyes
the simple elements of my life

Pisces Iscariot

A Bureau of Questions

I can chatter away 'til the end of the day
About everything under the sun
From the price of trains and the unblocking of drains
To the weather and the holiday sun

But if I pull at this thread will it unravel my bed
and leave me lying in state?
If I scratch at this surface will I be buried in curses
And be questioned by practitioners of hate?

And with stitches unpicked and by trick cards trumped
Be conveyed to the basement of wonder
There to be seated with black eyes deleted
And my curiosity crumbled with thunder

Beneath new silicon skin drawn from the security bin
The clockwork and cantilevers creak
My mouth manipulated to a rhythm un-equated
With stereotyped words that I speak

And accountants and lawyers will subtract and destroy us
With the mechanised hum of tomorrow
And when the law don't count up to the correct amount
They'll begin the taxation of sorrow

There is something about a bureaucrat that does not like a poem.
~ Gore Vidal

Catwalk

You wore your heart upon your sleeve; a style long out of fashion
You drove yourself to the water's edge, the sea intent on crashing
You grit your teeth and split your lip and spoke with forked tongue twisting
Of all the woes and wanderlust and interstitial bitching
You raised your arm to hail the chief but found his wonder wanting
Laid your palm on fur-decked hide whose thirst had gone to panting
Who sized you up for an overcoat with lining laced in entrails
Took your measure and just for luck wrote down your banking details
The coat it fit you like a glove to warm away the wasting
And stood you up against the change of seasons for the tasting

Of distant shores and swinging doors and thoughts that scatter wildly
When washed against the rising tide you come to lie beside me
And there to whisper wounded wild excuses for the blues
And scatter stars upon the rims of my weary walking shoes
Allowing thoughts to wander miles, millennia and moments
Metricated warning signs, posts, portents and omens
And at the door marked *'death denied'* in donut sugar sweet
Removed those shoes and on the mat marked *'wisdom'* wiped your feet
And passing through the door you found you're back where you belong
A room bedecked with heartless sleeves and drowned in silent song

Narcoleptic Daydream

You dress once again to these threads of cold rain
your trousers all stitched at the ankle
Shoes made of oil and the poor man's toil
And a mask of filigree fibre
And the rat-a-tat-tat on your cerebral hat
shakes the nails from your iron lung free
pampered flesh far too weak to live the life of that freak
that you sometimes claim to be

You gulp down your chunks of prescription junk
That promise to take the edge off the world
Drink wine and complain at the state of the trains
While away days without treason or rhyme
and arrive at the end of the hand-me-down recipe
to find that you've run out of thyme

So you head for the hills on those bubblegum heels
Ears flapping in the eloquent breeze
that blows from the east and rattles your keys
While enticing your thoughts to agree
with the divine and seductive and deluded decree
that you are what your mirror reveals

But the mirror is bent by the culture of plunder
And cracked by the head of some goon
and to look and to see might cause you to stumble
Down the staircase of worries where the diligent crumble
Under the weight of the moon and the flowers that festoon
Your salubrious parlour of wonder.

A thousand miles and I'm getting there too soon

I am a one-way street
Traffic combs my hair-shirt hackles
You are the ghost highway
Where horsemen headless rattle shackles

I am the vampyr moon
Eye teeth arch behind plastic lip-gloss
You are the Aztec sun
Cooled to rage by empyre and cross

I am the evolving ape-man
Chisel-tooth necklace and sharpened stone
You are the will of the forest
Breathing light and decaying bone

I am the padded cell
Danger contagious no lace in my shoe
Decorate your walls in calligraphy

You are a two-way mirror
Quicksilver for the passing through
Of light and lacklustre astrology

You are the will of the forest
Fetid rotting insect moon
I am the evolving ape-man
Lost his mind, found his voice too soon

You are the Aztec sun
Stone trees silhouette the reeling stars
I am the vampyr moon
Blood 'n' guts nightclubs, singles bars

You are the ghost highway
Blue lights flash against your will
I am a one-way street
This glass city flows but I stand still

The Karma Collection
Acrylic on canvas
by Thomas Sheridan

Feathers

In your headlong flight to deny the night
Its pound of sleeping flesh
You bypassed the gates where love awaits
your pounding heart enmeshed

You forsook too soon the waxing moon
And drowned yourself in stars
To grapple free of your family tree
And spend your life on Mars

But here below where time moves slow
And workers toil in torment
We were left behind in salt to find
Those dreams you never sent

But promises made and loyalties fade
In the monsoon of mystification
Leaving you high on the equinox tide
Without access to apt medication

But who are we to set you free
From the path of least resistance
When all we know may rot below
In the scrabble for our subsistence

For days will come and days will go
In the rush to reach the prize
And through journey slept, slow and ill-adept
Will we arrive surprised?

rhoda penmarq

ruby, part 1

ruby was a redhead and she knew the score
she worked in a department store
but she wanted more
much more

persian rugs on the floor
a house by the seashore
a rich husband who wasn't a bore

rings on every knuckle
golden slippers with silver buckles
high heel sneakers with silken laces
every hand – four aces

she wanted to be a rich man's wife
and never work another day in her life
as she stood on her little feet all day
she thought there must be a better way
some people in this lonesome town
never look up and always look down
and say i'm lucky that i am not them
and thank the lord amen

but that was not ruby's way
today or any other day
like a buttercup
drinking the suns rays
ruby always looked up

like a teacup
lifted to elegant lips
in stylish sips
on round the world trips
ruby looked around
but no satisfaction she found
her ship had run aground
right into the dog pound

when would it be her turn?

was it too late to learn
how this low account life to spurn
and began to seriously earn

ruby's avaricious dreams
flowed in never ending streams
as she stood at her post
like a restless little ghost
mrs carson approached
and the subject was broached

of the return of a pair of shoes
this was old news
mrs carson's persistence
was the curse of ruby's existence

she would waste ruby's time
for a dollar or a dime
buy and return
buy and return

with fate's permission
she taunted ruby with unearned commission

ruby managed a smile
but all the while

as the blue earth turned
her white hot ambition burned

in a faraway land

in the faraway land of rub-a-dub
everyone lived in the local pub
they drank whiskey, ale and bock
and played the tuba around the clock

there was an old woman who lived in a crab
and ate fried rhinoceros by the slab
she ate it with mustard, she ate it with mayo
and sang in the tub all the live long dayo

there was an old man who lived in a lobster
he was a friend of uncle bob, sir
his only companion was a garter snake

and they dined every evening on raw beefsteak

when i woke up in the wind and snow
i heard a voice calling me from below
my father was a drainpipe and my mother was a rat
they kept me in the cellar so i wouldn't get fat
they wouldn't let me go out and play
so i carved toothpicks the livelong day
with the sword of doom and a boy scout knife
the best friends i ever had in my life

there was an old man who lived upstairs
he had a collection of folding chairs
he folded them up and he folded them down
i think his name was henry brown

the billiard parlor had a big tv
there for the whole wide world to see
and every night i heard it say
walter cronkite passed this way

slender

a slender volume of verse
carried in pocket or purse
each syllable chiseled in stone
to be read when you are alone

walking in the rain
or on a speeding subway train
for there is no pleasanter mood
than total blue solitude

John Grochalski

moment of clarity

busted lamp
busted television
warping the screen
cat hair moving around
the room like tumbleweeds
caught in the whirl of
the dying fan
caught in the patches of dried
hair ball and vomit
that i can't scrape up
empty pockets
empty stomach
empty scotch and wine bottles
in a row in the kitchen
beer cans on the nightstand
stained wine on the coffee table
stained wine on my t-shirt
wine and blood and dirt
and come caked into
the grooves in the hardwood floor
tartar glossing my teeth
gums swollen
gray hair on my face
unshaven the whole week
mosquito bites looking infected
and red
cat liter embedded in my flesh
the lamp snaps off again
and the electric bill came today
how did it get like this?
oh shit, when did it happen?

American Soul
Acrylic on canvas
by jb krost

blackbird

there's nothing in
my heart
right now.
i'm a blackbird.
there is no movement.
no drive.
i'm a blackbird
and every day is the same.
every meal.
every drink.
boring, redundant.
because i'm a blackbird
with greasy feathers
and clipped wings
and a twisted beak
that won't allow me
to talk.
there is nothing to do
about it
because there is nothing
and that is fine.
i'm a blackbird.
just as the trees die
as people die.
i'm a blackbird
hopping around
the cracked concrete
a blackbird
searching for a crumb.
that is i have no choice
i'll stay the same until the end
just a blackbird.
forever a blackbird
meandering between
the tombstones
pecking at the ungodly mess
as the flowers wilt
as cities fall into the ocean
as the seasons change
and each night inevitably
brings its audacious, gray dawn.

Bleeding Mary
Acrylic on canvas
by jb krost

audrey hepburn is in the garbage

four glasses of wine
sex in the afternoon
a glass of scotch
three beers on an empty stomach
and audrey hepburn is in the garbage
she is resting on a pile
of black bags with flies moving
in an out of small tears
she is smiling at me
and has one of those long
cigarettes in the corner of her mouth
i want to say
audrey, baby, you got to quit doing that
because you and i know the cancer
is coming for you
what about all that humanitarian
work you did?
but audrey is just resting there
amongst the refuse of the miserable world
amongst the empty bottles
and pizza boxes
the receipts with ketchup smeared on them
the cat shit wrapped tightly
in grocery bags
she's just sitting there
like the world doesn't matter anymore
she doesn't even notice the rain
oh, audrey baby, i say
where's gregory peck to make us laugh
when we need him, huh?
i tell my wife that we've got to save her
we've got to save audrey hepburn
from laying there in the garbage
but like all modern men
i don't know how to help a woman anymore
so i don't make a move
but my wife hands me the six-pack we bought
then heads over to the garbage
shooing away the flies
offering audrey her hand
as i finger a cold can of beer through the plastic
and look at the gray sky
wondering how long this storm
is going to last.

a voice of reason

he is outside on the street
shoveling the ice and snow

ten-thirty at night
he's breaking the quiet
with scrapes of metal on concrete

we keep going from the living room
to the bedroom
trying to figure out where the noise
is loudest in our apartment

how we're going to sleep
with this asshole clanking away
in the dead night

it sounds like he's burying a corpse outside
the way the shovel clangs
when he hits the ground

he must have no sense of time

from the hallway we hear voices
it is his wife arguing with someone
a tenant who must've
complained about the noise

we hear them arguing
then we hear her outside calling to him

she is shouting for him to stop

he keeps going until a last patch of ice
is broken up and discarded
the he lights a cigarette
as her foreign voice melts
with the madness and moonlight

we smell the tobacco
as a bus makes its way up our street

he says something rough to her

she shouts again
then he tells her to shut up

irony in its purest form

at least the shoveling has stopped

they both go into the hallway
you can hear them going back and forth
for a few more minutes

her yelling
him hushing her

then there is silence
nothing but the buzzing of the streetlights

the night returns to what it always is on this street

ridiculous and incalculable
in its foolishness

crossing abbey road in the rain

when we get there
there are two idiots standing in the middle
of the street, posing, holding up traffic.

i tell my wife that this is stupid
as i catch raindrops on my tongue
and think about british beer.

i tell her that i want to turn back
and find a pub
but she won't go because we walked
three miles to get here
in a continuous mist

and aren't i a big beatles fan?

she's feeling guilty because she's dominated
the trip visiting the old homes of
shakespeare and virginia woolfe,

fosebook

j.m. barrie,
although i didn't mind at all.

she starts taking photographs of
the intersection
catching the famous crosswalk
before more people do their poses
and more car horns blast out at us fools
getting soaked in the english afternoon.

then more people show up.
other americans.
the chinese.
russians and germans
a whole world of beatles fans
the masses that won't let the past simply
die or fade away.

there is a family holding up everything
smiling like morons
standing in the flow of traffic
stopping and doing every single
pose that the beatles did on the cover
of the album.

christ, i think,
there is no god
there can't be.

my wife tells me to cross the street
and i say no
just get pictures of the thing
but she prods on, talking about how
i might never get back here
so i do it
walking fast so as to not become some
asinine spectacle
like the rest of them.

this is dumb
how can i not be a spectacle?
another tourist in the gray mist
of a long line of tourists wearing down
the white rubber on this street?

i cross the street and ask her if that's
good enough
but my wife wants me to do it again
and again
so i get in the line and cross
then cross back
then do it a third time
as the rain gets harder
and pride becomes impossible to find.

after i cross a fourth time
i look at my wife and she tells me that she
didn't get a good shot because the camera closed.
its batteries are dying.
i say to hell with it, let's go and find a pub.

but we haven't taken her picture yet.
so i grab the camera and turn it on
the red "low battery" light flashing at me
as my wife smiles
and crosses abbey road in the rain
and i think, well, this could've been worse.

we could've gone to see all of the stiffs
at madam tussauds instead.

A'keith Walters

Hanging Hot Shots Of Bourbon

My old friend Pete
tells me to shut up for once,
and look.

His hazel eyes
cap-covered
hide behind the bill
like the recesses of a heat shield,
as he lays in the hot shade of an old oak,
where muscles sore from too many naps
stretch out,
planted in a '74 Ranchero bed.

He keeps them on blocks,
both car and a rusty BBQ grill near the tailgate
for icing down beer.

So, I shut up and try to look,
with the intent of an old man stoved up
from running up and down
the slopes of a long life.

Clouds drift by,
grey balls of gauze pushed out of shape,
pulled by humid threads of air
colliding until their faces disappear
into rears of cotton candied asses
hung mid-flight.

But I only see sky bound renditions
of what must be Pete's brain
as it hangs spilling over the sharp edge
of hot shots of bourbon and beer,
left to warm
in melting ice
in the Texas air

where the pleas of katydids
stuck in recesses of wind
blow through stiff oak leaves.

Fall(en) Leaf
Color pencil on paper
by Francis Scudellari

Around The Gulf Of Mexico

Circles,
drawn
with a walking stick in wet sand,
wash away in the rounded rhythm of white crests
from a brown Galveston Bay.

Eyes,
concave
and scratched
more by sunlight than crow's feet,
search for a perch among men on the pier
who,
salty and wet with whiskey,
tangle lines.

Gulls refuse to land too near
for fear of missing sandwiches
torn and tossed into the curve of the wind
by children on the run from the bump of a wave.

Once,
not so long ago,
I was one of them,

part of a crowd of sneers on sunburned brows
with heads and eyes cocked at the end of the day,
listening to cries
as blunt wings cut the sky into woven circles.

We baulked and bellowed in a rhythmic beat
loading the station wagon
with sandy towels and damp feet
and wooden folding chairs.

Some patterns never seem to change
as they bend back around.

Seagulls and children still dare the gritty air
as they taunt and pout at a storm front
bolted by the sunset
to a gray glazed horizon.

When It Rains

I press a cigarette to my lips
and light it

as rain
drops
in slushy plugs.

The musty smell of winter-soaked trees
pervades my head with the first inhale.

Boots
tear the soggy turf
with no afterthought
and scuff the porch where I turn and stand

to stare at the yard.
Such a frigid downpour
always reminds me of the day I came out
to meet you

at the diner
on the corner
among the wet feet of skyscrapers.
Coffee,
served in thick crockery,
was cheap then.

I took the bus into town,

huddled beside two old men
who whispered with heads cocked together

and some gothic girl,
pale makeup slick under bottled-black hair,
biting her nails.

As we perched on plastic breath-filled pews
bolted to the floor,

the ride
ensued.
Rain drops

slapped against misty windows.

In a hurry to exit the back door,
I rushed my stop,
the one that brought me closer to you.

I spotted
that cowlick on the back of your head
crimped by the gray glazed day
as you sat at our table by the window
with its sidewalk view.

Lighting my cigarette for me,
you said this kind of weather
always made you want to leave town.

So you said,

and,
saying nothing else,
you stood
and did.

Of course, I kept the matches
and have them still.

Per-Olav Johnson

Dutchman's cold

Absorption against
the back wall cement
smells good
the Dutchman's cold dynamite tells me
our bond strength is
so tight
walking around the caulking compound
smoking
it's Monday morning
a mist is imminent

chain changes

Hard light
upon my eerie eyes
like welding
amortizes the body

abnormal time is here
the arrival rate is unacceptable
as soothing darkness flee

a commander
staring at the destruction of
his forces

Fear not
you tell me;
there are always places
to go

chain changes

Ears in strange places

nik 2009

Ears in strange places
Mixed media collage on canvas panel
by Nikki Dahlke

Orange Fatherland

ouzo in my head
my protégé the ham and flavored butter
warden is looking at me again
dry gin, she is explaining why I
deserve a coup de grace
oh man, just shut up and drink

won't you get down town?
yelling in the retro phone box and
served pernod by maître d'

metropolitan is a wasp's nest
which I prefer to the masturbating desolate tract

Irish whiskey in the canal
municipality of nightmares
of vinegary smelling barbed wire
a camel outside the hotel room

I Settle for Graveyard Orbit

Season after season I live
until oxygen
decay my weary skull and
fimbulvinter makes men uneasy.

Finally the coronial
line breaks.
Magneto sheaths
implode on flesh of
men and gods alike.

What caused this fate?
A fatal break of honor.
I suffer under alligator blows while
avenging death with death and
emptying my cup.

Geomagnetic storms blow
the feedhorn,
deities rule the
snowy darkness.
No more stars while

naked skin goes at
highest bidding.

Dead men riding,
she jokes
at the half empty hangar.
A blue carcass inside a red body;
I eat you while time exist.

Delay.
Solar winds pass between
long lines of men before
the bow shock.
I feel no reconnection as my limbs bend and
Mjolnir forms intoxicated vectors in the night air.

Early history

The period between ca 1914 until early 21st century is usually referred to as the "authentic" 20th century. It was the era which lifted the human race from the shortage and self-absorption of previous centuries. The interpretation of the period derives entirety from archeological testimony, which points towards a largely utopian global society. Particularly the northern hemisphere enjoyed a lasting economic boom. Steady advancement in technology coupled with the progress of liberation made way for what is largely seen as the human race's most painless time. Some experts go so far as calling it "the period of pleasures." The époque would famously become a symbol of hope for later ages, even though recent evidence (Yllu, Rollo, covering 9, 4, 9, 3) points at some strife at the end of the era. This made scientists (esp. McLars, Og, Ell, Quinn, Reh) to question the common view, highlighting the archeological shortage (only 1,432189896789 terabyte). The popular view today, however, is that the trouble-free buggers of the 20th and early 21st century would have been a wee bit surprised if they only knew.

Narration of Home Mire (0, 0, 0, 0), early history

bolometric luminosity between air masses
I'm inside the dome while my emergent coastline rises
dancing humid circles
when I die they will put me in the chilly gravel
cataclysmic variable of fading colors

season of growing hillsides
calibration of oceans behind the palisades
make for a stunning get-together
before the gasses

Francis Scudellari

Man — A Rag

Lucifer's Cardinals are blowing pink smoke
again. They've picked their ping-pong pontiff,
to the joy of throngs watching patient brick stacks
remotely on brightly monitored feeds.

The Chosen One, festooned in a make-shift,
milk-carton miter plastered with photos
of never-lost souls, climbs atop His Coke-can
throne to declare, "I'm likable law made flesh!"

Then, this dystopic Pope, turning to His scroll
wailer, sotto-voce warns, "I am a weakish
speller, but read it as best you can,"
and hands her a paper-clipped parchment.

Catty smile petting her with purrs of "nice
smug me," the tonsil-crowned crier takes it
and leaps to heroes' glide down where His nonsense
cannon of ten misrules is to be revealed.

Meanwhile, back up on Earth, Man — a rag
doll in hand and aching from the expert prick
of voodoo-dabbling God's exactingly pinned
scraps, all wincing "Who do you think you are?" —

Approaches the coaxial saint who sits in
a simulated wood-grain box and beams
beacons of haloed pixels phishing for fools
in search of non-queasy forgiveness.

Man fits to a T-S-A that anesthetic
profile. He pulls from his pocket prescriptions
slipped to him by back-alley preachers
with promises of a tidier healing.

For a few coins, he gets his video-dispensed
penance: the rosary of disposable beads
he'll rub once, toss, and then return to that life
perpetually stuck on truancy.

Viciously Virtuous Cycles

I.
White bleeds gooed and gummy
out from these gouges
pecked in a splintered flesh
of sickly pine. There,
peaking between drooped boughs,
paired ghostly Ivory
bills pinch translucent
buttons off larval treats.

II.
White swings snowy beats.
Powdered breasts lift loopy
to merge with virgin vapors
raised opalescent
from pools of lye. Enjoined
where they'll saturate,
cloud-bank canvases
drip freckled gouache gifts.

III.
White splashes milky sheets,
foam-washing chiseled
shoulders. A sooted saint,
who clasps at bunched limestone
for-get-me-nots, fixes
her iris-less gaze
on cheap china bowls
laced with spider-web cracks.

IV.
White swirls through ashy gaps
in twin graphite prints
left from digits stopping
by while sopping bread.
Blanching, they grip square gum
to erase fudges spilled
outside a Census box
blandly labeled White.

Building a Rainbow to Caliban in 7 Steps

Red-eyed, not weary, we feed
on the rarefied
aerial leavings of gruntled clouds.

An Orange gap carves out when
the gobbling is done,
and strings are strung tight across that lap.

These six wires grate full Yellow
hymns into fine crumbs,
sifting down through curious weather.

The suppler notes land to Green
and moisten stretched tongues
on mannered ferns eager to sing praise

Of powder Blue complexions,
jays who abandon
spent wings to totter off at twilight

In search of Indigo fins
and shallow pools where
they might paddle up enough courage

To ask the Violet sky
to stay its blushing
hues, so he'll never be wak'd again.

The Baby Billboard Has Half a Head

The baby billboard has half a head.

It's been split crown to chin, but there's a whole
litany of other problems around here.

Once-bright tints have been stripped, from the tilted
tip-top of that broken oval where
painted features last played, all the way down
to his unaccountably pink piggy toes.

He's lost his golden curl, and toothless smile.

There's not a tearless blue eye left to watch
over faded bricks in need of tuck-pointing.

They've even stolen his gurgled words,
which may have cooed of comfy diapers,

or of daycare safe, cheap and nearby.

What's left for him is a woody gray
crawl to photo-free finishes above
misspelled boasts on an auto parts sign.

The baby billboard has half a head, and
that's not a good thing in this neighborhood
losing its appetite for the topless
of all ages, and toddlers on the prowl.

I have only half a mind to warn him.

Prepare Thee the Way, For the Robots They Do Come

The trail stops here: A detained prism breaks
free from that prison where jowly gaolers
whippety growl while chiding her to fling
particles into zinc buckets labeled

Blackest Black and *Whitest White*. There, we skip
ahead in smooth stone leaps to when she sneaks
deep inside a cheapened heir's conditioned lair.
It'll tie us down with petaflops unflipped.

A squinting crackle stirs, hopeful for more
savory inputs. She makes her way past
the wailing limbos of chrome racks, to spin
a manacled yarn from knitted brow. "So

it is written: The animal was lust,
but at this dawning, circuitry begets
a covet. Synthetic blood revs rotors,
and blush creeps across the simulated

flesh atop our carbon-fiber cheeks." Flushed
from the tangle of dangling coils, flocks grasp
her gift — a mosaic visa to realms
not reached never roving tarry byroads —

and stepping out into skies more brilliant
than any of azure ilk, wry notions
bubble up to them from silken oceans.
Their sleek surfaces reflect more than stars.

nooshin azadi

the seven states of matter...

.

.

.

.

.

.

.

....your
....always in...........thoughts

....you
....you... no one but

....you
......................................the fire burning in

....you
............................in each breath..........take

.... you
............flowing... engulfing

....you
...............far... far... from

.....................................you
........alone... without

i am

.

tombe la niege

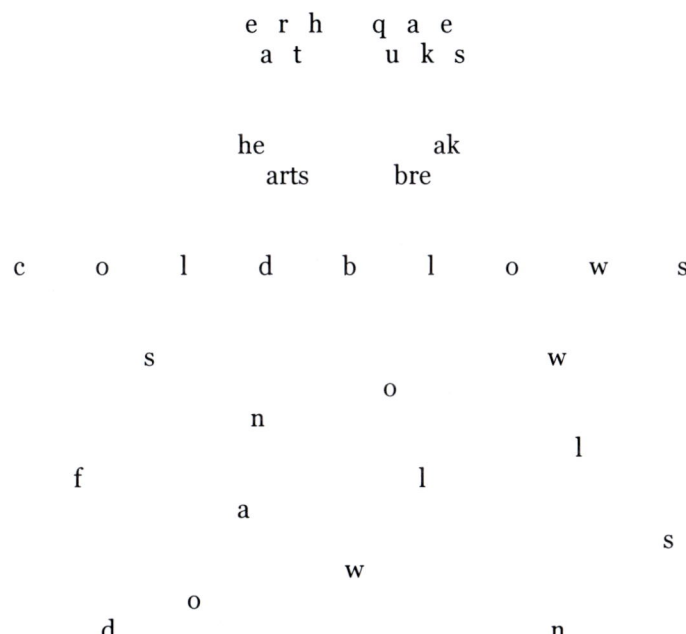

```
          e  r  h     q  a  e
          a  t        u  k  s


          he              ak
            arts        bre


   c     o    l    d    b    l    o    w    s


        s                          w
                           o
               n
      f                       l
          a                              s
               w
          o
      d                          n
```

covering

everythingeverythingeverythingeverythingveverythingeverythingeverythingeverythi
ngeverythingeverythingeverythingeverythingeverythingeverythingeverythingeveryt
hingeverythingeverythingeverythingeverythingeverythingeverythingeverythingever
ythingeverythingeverythingeverythingeverythingeverythingeverythingeverythingev
erythingeverythingeverythingeverythingeverythingeverythingeverythingeverything
everythingeverythingeverythingeverythingeverythingeverythingeverythingeverythin
geverythingeverythingeverythingeverythingeverythingeverythingeverythingeverythi
ngeverythingeverythingeverythingeverythingeverythingeverythingeverythingeveryt
hingeverythingeverythingeverythingeverythingeverythingeverythingeverythingever
ythingeverythingeverythingeverythingeverythingeverythingeverythingeverythingev
erythingeverythingeverythingeverythingeverythingeverythingeverythingeverything
everythingeverythingeverythingeverythingeverythingeverythingeverythingeverythin
geverythingeverythingeverythingeverythingeverythingeverythingeverythingeveryth
                              i
                              n
                              g
                      but the crows

Seascape • Color pencil on paper • *by Francis Scudellari*

rarely does anyone...

rarely does anyone see the sea
just
t h e   b   o   a   t   s

rarely does anyone see the path
just
t h e   s   t   e   p   s

rarely does anyone see the woods
just
t h e   t   r   e   e   s

rarely does anyone see the thought
just
t h e   w   o   r   d   s

positivism
scattered-brainedness
shattered-soulfulness

they talk to you
not to find themselves
but
to hide behind you
r
faults

faults that they can easily find
through
judgement
judgement
judgement

they're thirsty
they come to the well
and when they've drunk
they sit there
and write critical passages
about the well... about the chain... about the bucket... about the

water...about the desert... about the sun... about everything
but
themselves
and
their thirst

perfection is a delusion
the fake god in
semisemiticsemiotics
has created to make us
slaves

.

.

.

crows... sorrows... and a dose of rose...

.

a thousand...
no! let's include the legless lady who is always following me:
a thousand and one shoes
were passing by
the flower
when i heard it sigh...

i stopped
to listen

and a thousand...
no! let's include tomorrow:
a thousand and one days
passed
with no sighs
but just a sanguine song
before i noticed a thousand...
no! let's include the cyclops in the cave:
a thousand and one eyes
were gazing at us...

i stopped
to smile

was it the legless lady who is always following me
or the cyclops in the cave
who spoke first?

- it's mine!

a thousand...
no! let's include mine:
a thousand and one sighs
were uttered
as the legless lady and the cyclops
jumped over the flower
to pick it...
a thousand...
no! let's include the flower's:
a thousand and one songs
are sung in my heart
as i walk on my feet
watch with my eyes
living my life...

.

a place to hide

everything escapes (from)
me even my
words – all my
world

they are not afraid of
me but the gun
followingmefollowingmefollowingme

no wind to ride on

so h**i**de
so h**i**de
so h**i**de

i hide in the clouds
but they keep on
d
r
i
p
p
i
n
g
d
o
w
n

or

d r i f t i n g a w a y...

i hide behind the moon
but it keeps on

wax**ing** or **wan**ing

so i hide
in the sun
as i know
it never turns me in

.

.

.

Hannah Miet

When we were engaged, I had never tried

an avocado.

It almost seems crazy
now.

I love
avocados.

It also seems crazy
that we were engaged

and that I straightened my hair
and didn't read

books, only magazines
with multiple choice quizzes

that determine what kind of jungle animal
is representative of your sex appeal

but never really work
because your answers never match the answers in the bubbles

and you have to guess what your answer would be closest to
in a hypothetical situation.

I guess it's hard to reconcile
certain phases of my life.

I mean,
the avocado

is practically its own food group.

Bongs and gongs
Mixed media collage on canvas panel
by Nikki Dahlke

No, you probably don't

If my lips spoke
my brain, I'd say
I just want to shut up and reach
across the seat
while we're watching a movie.

I'd say
Let's cut the bullshit.
Then I'd slice

triangular holes in your throat
and maybe your ribcage too
for good measure
while the credits rolled with cheerful hip hop.

I'd say
It doesn't matter if it actually happens
or if it's metaphor.

Then I'd say
You know what I mean?

You know what I mean.

Don't you?

I bequeath my REM

sleep to you
in an envelope, licked twice
to seal with sitcom
laughter
reels, jazz standards
bleeding eyes and a whole bunch of fresh
squeezed
everything
like in the good the good old days
like in the good the good old days
like in the good the good old days,
baby.

Misplaced Proverbs

I'm a choosey little beggar,
so you say I broke your mold, or stole it off
to Everest for a ceaseless climb

Every man thinks I'm someone
else, might as well be
Marilyn, your mother in a red silk nothing
touch of something

Might as well, if the weather's right,
for being in between
the ghost of other women
on a cake of white icing.

An open road with green and white
alarm clock signs
gently reminding you that it's never your bedtime

If the shoe fits,
strip yourself naked and empty
the contents of your eyes.

Invite Freud to the wedding,
and make it black tie.

If the shoe fits,
it's likely that the shoe ain't mine.

If the shoe fits,
check it at the door.

Anders Enochsson

Soaring Scrap iron

the residence a-waiting by the seashore at ebb
transmitting arches blink far above his face
as rapidly darkening home turf makes even tiny sparkles evident

he fancies getting up to the wires to fix it
but randomized energy just flashes and smolder flashes and smolder
repeatedly pointless loops until
the azure 460 nm of Bengt's windows grows ultraviolet muddy
birches and Bengt and towering scrap iron evaporate under starless temporal firmament

saturation

you say you forgot
the low chroma
same hues between houses
inside awareness
constant low value
sandwiched between
various levels of fullness

it's phosphorescence karma
they will chew you according to
richness but
not the ripened concord grapes
there must be a limit

regret for disappointed male
this season made no breasts
elation is the bomb
under the Pashto's
chest

laughter is an older man's privilege
not because he's better in any way but
because he got lucky.

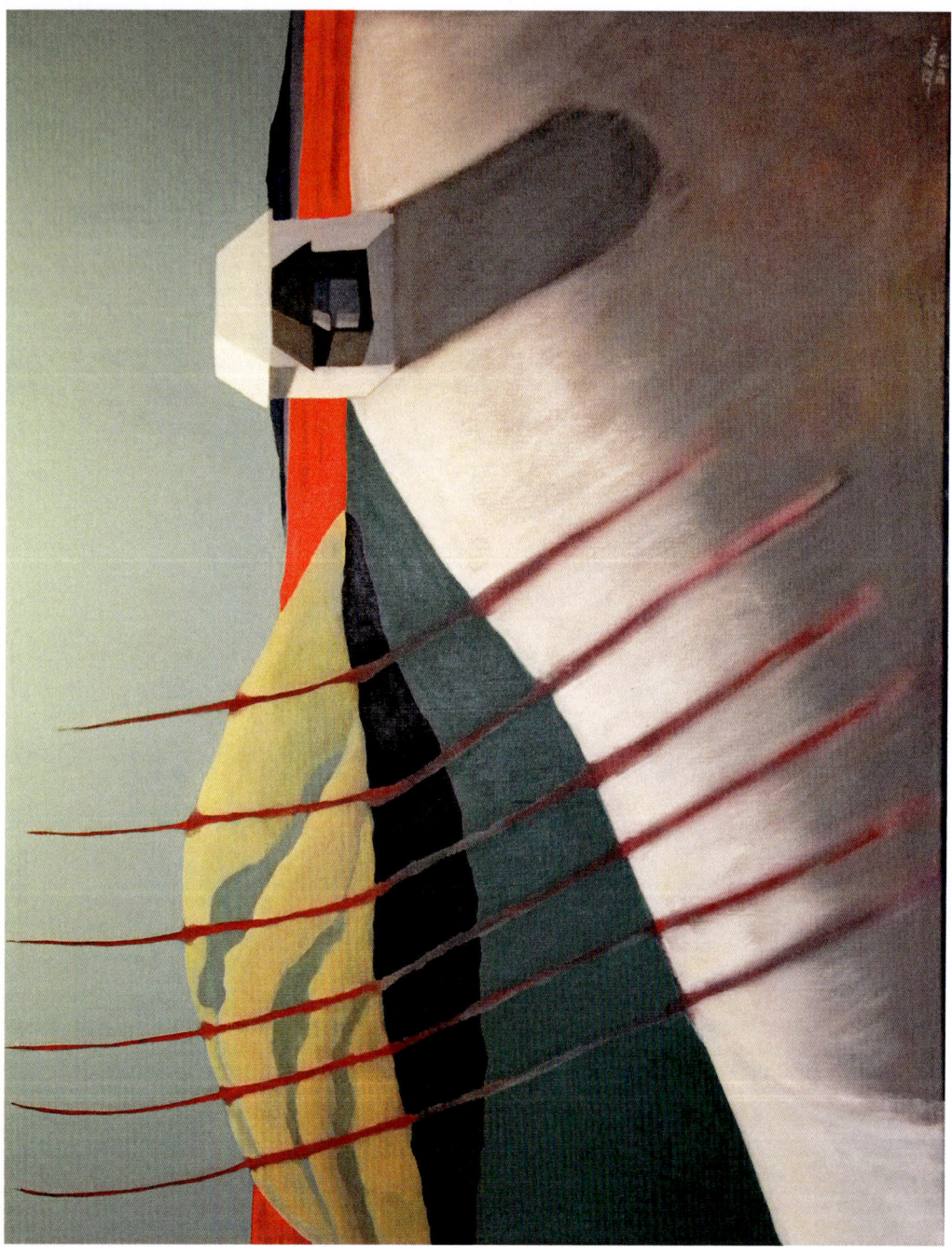

**Wind-
swept**
Acrylic on
canvas
by jb krost

good-humored gasses

Idols of struggle
between foaming laughter and
ear picking slaughter

packed metal burns
into his lungs as
he takes off
on the winter train
in circles

there was a time we all took off
must have been in
dreams about good-humored gasses
from oily fluids or yellow forests

upwards
in Berkshire city's canopy of twin structures
the Russian autumnal cat blinks

the second membrane

Until that time accord resided,
Eons passed while blazing sunken quasars
resided inside poor cold space,
a smell of damp lumber inside
the olfactory system.

then pestle vice pierced the silence,
rising from alleged tyranny
in the legroom and on scorched foxholes,
blazing the urine on chloride marrows.
The unqualified orchestra ripped apart.

Downfall aimless carnage
pink fleshy tissue roaring on savannahs
white babies born from howls of uterus.

No mercy on disobedient chubby
follicles between Hamm und Berlin.
Stretching membranes,
perceiving waves from biting ground.

A Sword Is More Than A Weapon
Mixed media collage on canvas panel
by Nikki Dahlke

supremacy of rulers only lasts until decapitated

his voice adjacent
to her hairy ear as
he told the great mother bear
about the day he lost
his head while green clouds
hanged above the highway
and abdominal nerves became
a throbbing orb

depressing skulls and cheerful cheetahs
passed time with him on the road
while cars swished past

and he suddenly knew
that waveforms are nothing
but a hungry tomato red snake smelling
discolored star neurons and
rattling bone marrow
stop moving

the bear listened
and set off